Vision
Mission
Total Quality

The Master Management Series

William F. Christopher
Editor-in-Chief

2

Vision
Mission
Total Quality

Leadership Tools
for Turbulent Times

William F. Christopher

PRODUCTIVITY PRESS

Portland, Oregon

Volume 2 of the *Management Master Series*.
William F. Christopher, Editor-in-Chief
Copyright © 1994 by Productivity Press, Inc.

Productivity Press
P.O. Box 13390
Portland OR 97213-0390
United States of America
Telephone: 503-235-0600
Telefax: 503-235-0909

ISBN: 1-56327-055-2

Book design by William Stanton
Composition by Rohani Design
Printed and bound by BookCrafters in the United States of America

Library of Congress Cataloging-in-Publication Data

Christopher, William F.
    Vision, mission, total quality : leadership tools for turbulent times / William F. Christopher.
        p.   cm. -- (Management master series ; v. 2)
    Includes bibliographical references.
    ISBN 1-56327-055-2
    1. Total quality management. I. Title. II. Series.
    HD62. 15.C52   1994
    658.5'62--dc20   94-27919
                                                                          CIP

98 97 96 95   10 9 8 7 6 5 4 3 2

On Becoming a Leader (pg.45), © 1990 by Warren Bennis, Inc. Reprinted by permission of Addison-Wesley Publishing Company, Inc.

— CONTENTS —

PUBLISHER'S MESSAGE

The *Management Master Series* was designed to discover and disseminate to you the world's best concepts, principles, and current practices in excellent management. We present this information in a concise and easy-to-use format to provide you with the tools and techniques you need to stay abreast of this rapidly accelerating world of ideas.

World class competitiveness requires managers today to be thoroughly informed about how and what other internationally successful managers are doing. What works? What doesn't? and Why?

Management is often considered a "neglected art." It is not possible to know how to manage before you are made a manager. But once you become a manager you are expected to know how to manage and to do it well, right from the start.

One result of this neglect in management training has been managers who rely on control rather than creativity. Certainly, managers in this century have shown a distinct neglect of workers as creative human beings. The idea that employees are an organization's most valuable asset is still very new. How managers can inspire and direct the creativity and intelligence of everyone involved in the work of an organization has only begun to emerge.

Perhaps if we consider management as a "science" the task of learning how to manage well will be easier. A scientist begins with an hypothesis and then runs experiments to observe whether the hypothesis is correct. Scientists depend on detailed notes about the experiment—the timing, the ingredients, the amounts—and carefully record all results as they test new hypotheses. Certain things come to be known by this method; for instance, that water always consists of one part oxygen and two parts hydrogen.

We as managers must learn from our experience and from the experience of others. The scientific approach provides a model for learning. Science begins with vision and desired outcomes, and achieves its purpose through observation, experiment, and analysis of precisely recorded results. And then what is newly discovered is shared so that each person's research will build on the work of others.

Our organizations, however, rarely provide the time for learning or experimentation. As a manager, you need information from those who have already experimented and learned and recorded their results. You need it in brief, clear, and detailed form so that you can apply it immediately.

It is our purpose to help you confront the difficult task of managing in these turbulent times. As the shape of leadership changes, the *Management Master Series* will continue to bring you the best learning available to support your own increasing artistry in the evolving science of management.

We at Productivity Press are grateful to William F. Christopher and our staff of editors who have searched out those masters with the knowledge, experience, and ability to write concisely and completely on excellence in management practice. We wish also to thank the individual volume authors; Cheryl Rosen and Diane Asay, project managers; Julie Zinkus, manuscript editor; Karen Jones, managing editor; Lisa Hoberg, Mary Junewick, and Julie Hankin, editorial support; Bill Stanton, design and production management; Susan Swanson, production coordination; Rohani Design, composition.

Norman Bodek
Publisher

1

ACT! BUT HOW?

There's a new road map to success for today's turbulent times:

Vision + Mission + Total Quality

It's an ever-changing route to consistent and continuing success in this ever-changing world we live in and work in. Dramatic problems. Hard-to-find solutions. Hard-to-see opportunities.

Struggling to survive and prosper, companies take dramatic actions:

- restructure

- downsize and rightsize

- delayer, demass

- reengineer

- divest

- acquire

- form strategic partnerships

...and look for other executive actions to get on a winning track.

Management also sees successes from a new management system—Total Quality Management (TQM). Executives today embrace TQM, but most of them, not firmly enough.

They more incline to the listing above. They seek an executive action solution. They'll likely find that something more is needed.

Success, continuing success, and constant and continuing improvement have to be created—in many steps, by many people, at many levels. Some big steps, even transformational, but widely shared. Many smaller steps at all levels, shared among the people at those levels. Total Quality can provide how-to-do-it methods. But a driving theme—a shared purpose—will be needed. Vision and Mission will be the starting point.

2

TOTAL QUALITY ISN'T WHAT QUALITY USED TO BE

Quality for years meant inspection. Inspectors examined and tested output to assure that only production meeting specifications would be delivered to customers. This method worked, but not well. One result was the Accepted Quality Level (AQL)—assurance that no more than X percent of output would be out-of-spec. But no assurance that customers would be satisfied.

Then statistical methods were developed to find variances as products were being produced. By taking needed corrective action, defects could be prevented. As reliance on statistical methods grew, the need for inspection declined. And in recent years many new techniques arose for improving manufacturing processes, assuring quality and reducing costs. Among these:

- advanced statistical methods
- process flow charting and analysis
- process management
- personal computers, networks, software
- CAE/CAD/CAM
- CIM

- NC, DNC, CNC

- cycle-time reduction

- benchmarking

- improved sensors

- programmable controllers

- value-added manufacturing (VAM)

- rapid setup (single-minute exchange of dies, or SMED)

- flexible manufacturing systems (FMS)

- stockless production (JIT)

- group technology

- robotics

- small lot production

- mistake-proof devices (poka-yoke)

- visual controls

- empowerment

- total employee involvement (TEI), suggestion systems

- participation (corrective-action teams, quality-improvement teams, quality circles, problem-solving teams, etc.)

- self-managing work teams

- training, training, training

The new methods improved quality, eliminated waste, reduced costs, motivated employees, satisfied customer expectations, built market share, and improved profitability.

We then found that many of the methods so successfully used in manufacturing can also improve quality and productivity in other areas of the business. In staff departments. In functional groups. In the executive suite. In all of those areas the accountants call "overhead"—a bad name for a lot of important work. Recently, quality and productivity improvement methods have been brought together into the new TQM management system. In TQM the best management practices in every work area combine to:

1. satisfy customer needs and expectations

2. reduce costs

3. continuously improve

TQM methods improve quality and productivity, reduce costs, and satisfy customers not only in manufacturing, but also in services, in nonprofits, and in government. But first, a motivating theme, a shared purpose, is needed.

Where do we start? What matters most? There are so many options. So many products, services, markets, customers, prospects. So many concepts. So many techniques. What is right for my company? For my unit or organization? Vision and Mission answer these questions.

Vision and Mission provide:

- focus

- direction

- goals

- measures

- motivation

- a community of interest and aspiration

Out of all that's possible, Vision says where we're going. Mission lays out the road map. TQM methods can then produce the results needed for company success. From Vision and Mission, Quality finds focus.

3

VISION

Vision sets a direction into the future. It says to everyone in the company, "This is what we're all about." A Vision is a short statement of the company's drive and direction. It's the essence of the company's competitive advantage, to be created and grown. All company members will be part of making it happen and all will benefit from the results. Some Visions:

NASA—Put a man on the moon by the end of the decade.

Henry Ford—Produce a car that everyone can buy.

Disneyland—Create a place for people to find happiness and knowledge.

Girl Scouts—Help a girl reach her highest potential.

Baxter Healthcare Corporation—Baxter will be the leading single source of products and services which help hospitals to achieve cost-effective, high-quality health care.

Lincoln Electric Company—To produce the best possible welding products at the lowest possible cost, in order to sell to an ever-increasing number of customers.

Ritz-Carlton Hotels—For every guest, a warm welcome, anticipate guest needs, and a fond farewell, from Ladies and Gentlemen serving Ladies and Gentlemen.

McCaw Cellular Communications—Provide an automatic call delivery system, connecting people to people, not to places.

Marriott—Grow a worldwide lodging business using Total Quality Management (TQM) principles to continuously improve preference and profitability. Our commitment is that every guest leaves satisfied.

GTE Automotive and Miniature Lighting—Sustain a leadership position in automotive and miniature lighting by providing the highest quality light sources and lighting systems at competitive prices.

I include in the listing above some Visions that go back decades. We might write some of these differently today. But as stated then, and as communicated and applied, they inspired their organizations to high achievement. And that is the purpose, and the value, of Vision.

Vision statements will be short, their concept broad, their direction clear. While the statement is simple, its creation is not. Vision statements can't be found from facts, data, reports, and analysis. Vision is about the future, which we don't yet know. Vision is Monday-morning quarterbacking before the game is played. It's how we'll play the game, being who we are, what we know and can learn, and how we see the future and the world around us.

Burt Nanus, in his book, *Visionary Leadership*, says:

"A vision is a realistic, credible, attractive future for your organization." *

Visions are created by leaders, not by managers. There is a difference, as we see in Table 1.

But a Vision that works to create a "realistic, credible, attractive future" does not belong only to the leader. It belongs to the whole organization. To everyone. It's a guiding light. A star to steer by. The leader creates a Vision that is right for the organization, sets the direction toward that Vision, and leads the organization through the changes needed to get there. The

* Burt Nanus, *Visionary Leadership* (San Francisco: Jossey-Bass, 1992, p. 8.

Table 1. Managers vs. Leaders

Manager	Leader
Administers	Innovates
A copy	An original
Maintains	Develops
Focuses on systems and structure	Focuses on people
Relies on control	Inspires trust
Short-range view	Long-range perspective
Asks "how" and "when"	Asks "what" and "why"
Has an eye on the bottom line	Has an eye on the horizon
Imitates	Originates
Accepts the status quo	Challenges the status quo
A classic good soldier	His or her own person
Does things right	Does the right things

Source: W. Bennis, On Becoming a Leader, Reading, Mass.: Addison-Wesley, 1989, p. 45. Reprinted by permission of Addison-Wesley Publishing Company, Inc.

visionary leader becomes a direction setter and a spokesperson, a change agent and a coach, as shown in Figure 1.

Looking outside the company, the visionary leader is a direction setter and a spokesperson; inside the company, a coach and change agent. In all four roles, the guiding banner will be the company vision. The right Vision for the organization:

- fits the organization and the times

- sets a standard of excellence

- clarifies direction and purpose

- inspires enthusiasm and commitment

- is clear and easy to understand

- evokes the unique competence of the organization to create competitive advantage

- is ambitious*

* Nanus, pp. 28–29.

How can the leader create such a Vision? Burt Nanus offers an eight-step process:

1. Take a good look at the company and its market position.

2. Examine organization values, strengths, weaknesses.

3. Assess present direction and momentum, and where these are leading.

4. Query company constituencies to understand their needs.

5. Identify future developments that could impact the company, build scenarios.

6. Generate alternative Visions from the previous steps.

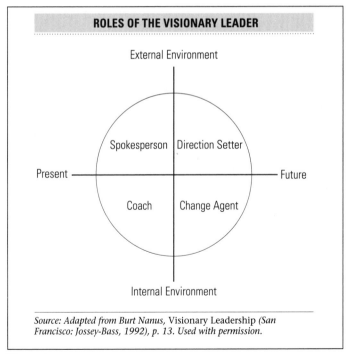

ROLES OF THE VISIONARY LEADER

External Environment

Spokesperson | Direction Setter

Present ———————————— Future

Coach | Change Agent

Internal Environment

Source: Adapted from Burt Nanus, Visionary Leadership (San Francisco: Jossey-Bass, 1992), p. 13. Used with permission.

Figure 1.

7. Select a Vision that best focuses company capability on external opportunity.

8. Involve a lot of people in every step.*

A Task Team of the CEO and senior executives can follow this eight-step process to develop a Vision that will be a driving force for their company. Once created, the Company Vision becomes its banner, a symbol setting direction for the future. The Vision Statement needs to be seen everywhere, all the time. It will be in company publications, on plaques and displays, on bulletin boards, in management reports, in stockholder reports and financial statements, in project proposals and requests for expenditure, in budgets and plans, in policy manuals and included in work standards—in all the places that are seen by company members in their daily work, and by other company constituencies in their contacts with the company. The Vision will be everywhere. All the time. Everywhere that words appear, there will appear also the Company Vision. On signs. On paper. On computer screens. On PA systems and telecommunications. Everywhere.

Vision sets direction, but something more is needed to embed the Vision in all company operations. What is needed, for all members of the company, is a clear translation of "what the Vision means for me." We all need to know, accept, and support our part in making the Vision real. Specific goals, measures, and actions are needed at all levels. All this can be created by a system of Missions.

---

* Burt Nanus, Part 2, pp. 43–129.

4

MISSION

Vision sets direction, but it does not provide a road map. It does not state what the company must do, and the results needed from each unit and work group. It does not lay out the measures at each level that provide feedback and chart progress. A system of Missions, created with member involvement, can spell out the needed performance and measures:

- First, a Mission for the total company, then...
- Missions for units and subunits of the company, to the level of work groups and processes.

Companies may use other words (Strategy or Business Plan) for what I call Mission. But, whatever the label, the content is what matters. What I call Mission is brief, understandable, complete—all that's needed to prescribe the actions and provide the measures that enable company people to make the Vision a reality. Missions are much shorter than most Business Plans and more specific than many Strategies.

COMPANY MISSION

As with Vision, finding and stating a Company Mission that will make the Company Vision a reality will need the involvement of many company people. A good method is to use the Vision Task Team of company executives perhaps aided in their work by an outside expert. Each of these executives can then form teams in their individual areas of work to assist in finding the Mission. In turn, the members of these second-level teams can talk with others in their work groups to describe the work of the Mission teams, and to get information and ideas. Since Mission is all about company operations—markets, products and services, relationships, goals, measures, and values—Task Team members will not be doing "more work." Instead they will be "doing their jobs," focusing and cooperating on what needs to be done to succeed, to move toward the Company Vision, now and into the future. Here are four steps for creating a Company Mission.

Step 1

At the first meeting of the Task Team, write down the Company Vision at the top of a sheet of paper. This Vision will be Item One of the Company Mission. Discuss the Vision. Explore needed actions. Assess the company today against its Vision:

- Where are we strong?

- Where must we do better?

- What must change?

Look at where we are and, as things stand now, where we're going. Is that strongly and surely toward our Vision? Is everyone involved?

From where we are today, the task is to spell out a Mission that will make the company Vision a reality. Vision is a destination. Mission is a road map. Mission includes all that's needed to guide the company to its Vision. Short. Clear. Complete. And inspiring! A good Company Mission will include these fundamentals:

1. *Vision.* The realistic, credible, attractive future for the company.

2. *Business definition.* If needed in addition to Vision.

3. *Goals.* The major goals to be reached in the Key Performance Areas or Success Factors that will determine company success.

4. *Measures.* Performance measures chart progress toward the goals, and provide feedback to help those doing the work achieve the goals.

5. *Values.* How the company lives and acts in all that it does.

Points 2 through 5 derive from Company Vision. So, first, write down the Vision. Think about it. Discuss what it means and where it leads. Then, everything the Task Team does should relate to and support the Vision.

Step 2

After writing down the Vision and assessing where the company now stands, the next step is to focus on the starting point for all company success:

- markets
- customers
- products and services, and the superior customer values provided to these markets and customers

Write down what these are today by appropriate groupings. Then write down what they will be in the company's Vision. Sounds simple. But this task will take time. Think carefully and creatively about what is written down. Markets can be described as product markets (computers) or as functional markets (information systems). Customers can be:

1. direct purchasers of company products and services

2. end users

3. potential customers for the product or product function.

4. all those in some way involved with or affected by company outputs of products and services

Products and services and customer values should include a statement of the competitive advantage—the unique value—the company will provide to its customers.

Money comes to the company from customers. So do profits, however measured in financial statements. Creating customers must be the focus and goal of business actions. And we create customers by totally focusing on the customers to be served, and satisfying their expectations in everything the company does. A companywide quality strategy is an effective way to focus actions on satisfying customer expectations.

For example, while working out a Vision/Mission/Total Quality road to its future, one company redrew its organization chart. The new chart is not lines and boxes. It shows customers and prospects as the focus for everything the company does (see Figure 2). All functions collaborate through the "Circle of Communication and Teamwork." Many company people in addition to sales personnel interact with customers to deliver satisfaction. These contacts are shown by the "focus" lines on the chart. Some go to the customers. Others go only as far as the Circle of Communication and Teamwork. Creating customers has become the focus of all company actions.

With this point of view, Vision/Mission/Total Quality created a high-performance organization that turned a three-year record of substantial losses into a new record of high profitability.

Step 3

Next, write down and think about all the other groups (constituencies) important in the success of the company, including:

- employees

- suppliers

- shareholders

- communities in which the company operates

- government

• the natural environment

• the industry the company is a part of

First come employees. But, please, use a more realistic term, such as:

• Members

• Associates

• Partners

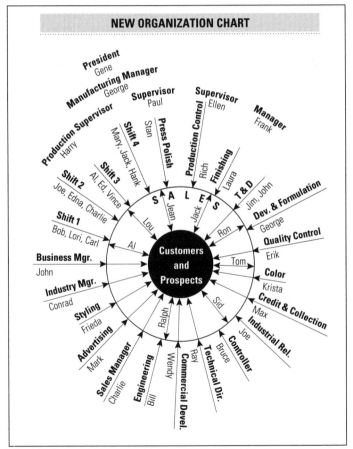

Figure 2.

The people working for the company create what the company is and what it becomes. Everybody—executives, workers, managers, professionals—is an employee, a member, an associate, a partner. Let's recognize this oneness in the terms we use.

Listing and thinking about these constituencies will carry further the work done in finding the Company Vision. These are groups involved in company success. Each contributes. Each has expectations. For each one, stand in their shoes and from their viewpoint answer three questions:

1. How do they define company success?

2. What are their expectations from the company?

3. What are their responsibilities to the company?

For insight, Task Team members may wish to talk to some constituents about these questions. However, enough information to create the Mission will be found in the collective heads of Task Team members and the other company people they talk to.

To find and create the Mission, most important is what we know and what we learn about:

- products

- services

- technology

- today's markets, and customer needs and expectations

- tomorrow's markets and customers, and their needs and expectations

- external social and environmental relationships

- company capability

We create success by the competitive value we deliver to customers in the context of the world we work in. All else flows from this.

Burt Nanus's eight-step process for finding Vision mentioned earlier leads also to the Company Mission. The information from the steps for finding Vision also fold into the process for spelling out the Mission. Company Vision is the successful future. Company Mission is the way to get there.

Step 4

Write the Mission Statement. From the knowledge and experience of Task Team members, and from what is learned in steps 1, 2, and 3, we can find a Mission with the goals and measures that will move us toward the Company Vision. We'll know, agree on, and get excited about what we need to do now to make the Vision real. In six pages or less, the Company Mission—the road map to Vision—will state the Company Vision and then the basic guidelines toward the Vision:

- business definition
- goals
- measures
- values

WRITING THE COMPANY MISSION

STATE THE COMPANY VISION

Everything the company does will strive toward this Vision.

BUSINESS DEFINITION

Business definition is a brief statement of the business the company is in, stated broadly enough to include areas of opportunity the company may enter in the future. Good business definitions will include three elements:

1. products and services to be offered

2. markets and customers to be served

3. special customer values offered by the company that will build customer relationships and create competitive success.

When the Company Vision includes these points, it is not necessary to write an additional business definition. Only when it is felt that additional information is needed should a more complete business definition be included in the Company Mission.

GOALS

Vision paints a picture of the company's future. To reach this future, success will be determined by results in a few Key Performance Areas (KPAs) or Success Factors (SFs). Specific goals can be set for each KPA/SF. To achieve its Vision (see page 7), GTE Automotive and Miniature Lighting set five major goals:

1. Pursue leadership in quality, cost, and technology

2. Increase market share

3. Provide profits for continued investment and stockholder return

4. Provide a safe, professional work environment for employees

5. Be a good corporate citizen

Goals, and the measures of progress toward the goals, will be the guiding road map toward the Company Vision. Goals will be needed in the Key Performance Areas/Success Factors that matter most in reaching the Company Vision. For most companies, these KPAs/SFs will include:

1. *Sales and Market Position.* Goals can be stated for sales revenue, market share, competitive position.

2. *Innovation.* Vision is a picture of change. Goals are needed for making and marketing new products and services; and for change and improvement in company processes.

3. *Quality and Productivity.* Goals are needed for satisfying customer expectations; eliminating error and waste; and for improving output in relation to inputs of person-hours of work, materials, energy, and capital.

4. *Profitability.* Profit goals are needed to provide investment funds for creating the company's future and to reward shareholders.

Company operating success will be measured in all four areas—not in profitability alone. Profitability results from what we achieve in the first three. So let's concentrate on these driving forces. A total of four to eight goals in these four KPAs can clearly show what the company must do now to reach its Vision. To reach these goals, the company has two powerful resources:

- its people
- its balance sheet assets (capital)

People working with capital produce results. So these are two more KPA/SFs:

5. *Leadership of People.* Goals can be set for the growth and development of company people, and for the structure of company work.

6. *Management of Capital Resources.* Goals can be set for how capital is acquired, maintained, and managed so that people working with capital will achieve the company's performance goals.

And our business is not alone. It is part of an economy, a society, a natural environment that it must relate to and support. A seventh KPA/SF where goals are needed:

7. *Public and Environmental Responsibility.*

A total of eight to twelve major goals in these seven Key Performance Areas/Success Factors can clearly and fully describe the Company Mission that will move the company to its Vision.

One of the seven areas is titled "Quality and Productivity." But the ideas and methods of Total Quality Management will be used in all seven areas to produce the needed results. Among these ideas and methods:

- focus on customers, external and internal

- process: definition, analysis, management, and improvement

- statistical methods

- mistake-proofing devices (poka-yoke)

- cycle-time reduction; time as a metric

- benchmarking

- participation, empowerment

- work teams

- system thinking

- customer-satisfying innovation

- continuous improvement

MEASURES

With goals set in each KPA/SF that will determine company success, measures are needed. Measures provide feedback. They tell us how we're doing in producing the results that will take us to our goals, and to our Vision. Measures give us information needed to:

- take corrective actions

- find and develop opportunities

Mission states the measure(s) of success for each of the goals.

Goals make Mission clear. They are tasks ahead. They are targets on the pathway toward the Company Vision. But goals are useful only when combined with measures. A goal without a measure is a target without a way to get there; a way to track and recognize performance. Measures motivate, when they are created and used by those doing the work. What's measured is what matters most. Mission measures are the measures of company success.

The Company Mission sets specific goals for the company in all the KPAs/SFs that can make real the Vision. And it states performance measures for each of these goals. These measures can then become the company's management information system. Separate from the financial reporting system, mission measures provide feedback on what's happening now that's needed for the day-by-day and month-by-month decisions and actions to reach the goals and achieve the Vision.

VALUES

In Mission, both "what" and "how" matter. Mission will state the kind of company we are and aspire to be. Our values. They way we work and deal with others. These statements must be us, the way we really are. Or, if there is stretch in them toward the way we want to be, we must take actions to make these changes happen. We must be and act as we state in our Mission. We must walk the talk. For competitive success in today's world, Mission values will be like those in the "New Culture" column in Table 2.

EXAMPLES OF MISSION GOALS AND MEASURES

Examples of Mission goals and measures are described in Table 3 (pp. 24–25).

1. The left column shows examples of Mission goals in the seven KPAs/SFs just described.

2. The right column gives useful measures for each goal.

The seven Key Performance Areas described fit most businesses well. But while different businesses may use the same KPAs, the goals and measures will differ. Businesses are different. And so will be their goals, measures, and information systems. Some will have KPAs different from, or in addition to, these seven. But the total number should be few.

The examples in Table 3 are selected from the author's experiences in working with over one hundred businesses in seventeen countries.

HOW TO MEASURE

The most useful Mission measures will not be the variance kind of measures used in financial reporting. Instead of

Table 2. Mission Values

CATEGORY	PREVIOUS STATE	NEW CULTURE
Customer Requirements	Incomplete or ambiguous understanding of customer requirements	Use of a systematic approach to seek out, understand, and satisfy both internal and external customer requirements
Suppliers	Unidirectional relationship	Partnership
Objectives	Orientation to short-term objectives and actions with limited long-term perspective	Deliberate balance of long-term goals with successive short-term objectives
Improvement	Acceptance of process variability and subsequent corrective action assigning blame as the norm	Understanding and continually improving the process
Problem-solving	Unstructured individualistic problem-solving and decision-making	Predominantly participative and interdisciplinary problem-solving and decision-making based on substantive data
Jobs and People	Functional, narrow scope management-controlled	Management and employee involvement; work teams; integrated functions
Management Style	Management style with uncertain objectives that instills fear of failure	Open style with clear and consistent objectives, which encourages group-derived continuous improvement
Role of manager	Plan, organize, assign, control, and enforce	Communicate, consult, delegate, coach, mentor, remove barriers, and establish trust
Rewards and recognition	Pay by job. Few team incentives	Individual and group recognition and rewards, negotiated criteria
Measurement	Orientation toward data-gathering for problem identification	Data used to understand and continuously improve processes

Source: "Total Quality Management Guide" (DOD 5000.51-G), Final draft, 2/15/90.

variances from plan or past performance, they will be measures of trend and changes in trend toward the goal. They show us:

- whether we are on track toward the goal

- where and when corrective action is needed

- where there is opportunity for improvement

The management information system of Mission trend measures empowers managers to lead by "predictive control," as shown in Figure 3.

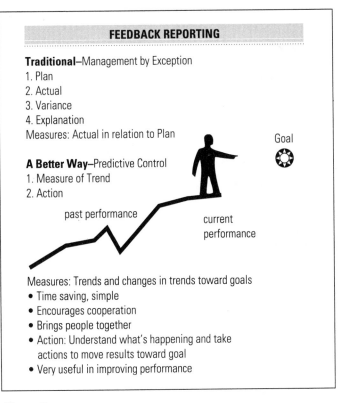

Figure 3.

Table 3. Examples of Goals and Measures

GOALS	MEASURES
For operating performance:	
KPA 1. Sales and Market Position	
a) Double sales revenue (constant dollars) within eight years.	a) 12-month moving total beginning five years ago and showing the 8-year target ahead
b) Be a market leader in each strategic business.	b) Listing of strategic businesses. For each, the market share trend charted quarterly. (If market share data not available, use marketing department assessment of market position in relation to the top six competitors.)
c) In each strategic business, create a competitive advantage that will win the major share of target client business.	c) Competitive position with key target clients
KPA 2. Innovation	
a) Create new products that will amount to 25% or more of sales revenue within five years.	a) Sales revenue from products and services new within last five years—dollars, and percent of total sales, charted in time series
b) Find new technology and methods to change and improve processes and reduce costs by $8.5 million per year.	b) Cost changes from process improvements reported monthly and cumulatively, year-to-date
c) Change the standard costing system to an Activity Based Cost Management system by December 31.	c) Project benchmark reports
KPA 3. Quality and Productivity	
a) Increase Value Added per Dollar of Payroll Expense by 5% a year.	a) 3-month moving average of value added per dollar of payroll expense
b) Zero defects shipped to customers.	b) Number of defects, daily
c) Increase Total Productivity 5% per year.	c) $\dfrac{O}{L + M + K + E + OOP}$ quarterly time series chart O—Output L—Labor (all employees) M—Materials K—Capital input E—Energy input OOP—Other outside purchases used (all measured in constant dollars)
KPA 4. Profitability	
a) Grow net income 8% per year, on trend.	a) 12-month moving total of net income, from five years ago and showing the annual 8% goals for eight years ahead
b) Invest new capital assets in support of Company Mission, with more than half of this investment in new technology.	b) Include Company Mission screen in RFEs; monitor: • Quarterly and annual totals, total new investment • Quarterly and annual totals, investment in new technology

c) Maintain profitability in the top quartile of the 25 largest firms in our industry.

c) quarterly report on the 25 largest firms listed in rank order by return on sales, and showing also: total sales revenue and net profit

KPA 5. Leadership of People

a) Receive and implement 5 suggestions per employee within two years, with a steadily rising trend thereafter.

a) Time series, reported monthly:
  - Number of employee suggestions
  - implemented, left scale
  - Implemented suggestions per employee, right scale

b) Establish gainsharing compensation plans that will include all company employees.

b) Quarterly report on
  - number of employees participating in gainsharing compensation plans
  - Project reports on plans begin developed

c) Provide at least 40 hours of training each year for all employees.

c) Quarterly report on hours of training and year-to-date totals by employee group

d) Establish and maintain an information system that provides the feedback needed by each work group and employee.

d) Project benchmark reports, Annual employee survey

KPA 6. Management of Capital Resources

a) Establish and maintain a system of Total Productive Maintenance in all operations.

a) TPM reports by plant, monthly

b) Find and invest in new process technology that will keep company operations World Class.

b) Annual technology audit

c) Improve capital productivity 2 1/2% per year, on trend.

c) Quarterly time series of the index of capital productivity from base year = 100, showing the goals for 2 1/2% annual improvement for eight years ahead. Capital productivity calculated as:

$$\frac{\text{Output}}{\text{Capital Inputs}}$$

Capital inputs = Depreciation + a selected interest cost of capital + operating costs of capital (maintenance, property taxes, property insurance)

KPA 7. Public and Environmental Responsibility

a) Contribute to the development of government regulations affecting the company, and fully comply with all government regulatory requirements.

a) Annual audit

b) Provide open communication with the media, and with other interested outside constituencies.

b) Annual audit

c) Support employee participation in community affairs.

c) Annual audit

d) Manage all company actions to conserve the environment.

d) Annual audit

Mission measures show progress toward goals. They give us information for needed actions. Time series and graphics provide understanding of change and trend, helping managers see developing problems and opportunities and take actions needed to achieve desired results. Predictive control aims to understand yesterday, and the internal and external environments and how these are changing. Using this information, we create tomorrow. We create the Company Vision.

Predictive control using this kind of reporting is a key concept of Total Quality Management. Know what's happening as it's happening, and take actions as needed to make what's happening produce the desired result. This kind of reporting and control is one of TQM's historical roots.

COMPLETING THE MISSION STATEMENT

The Mission Task Team could work forever to come up with a Mission that is really right for the company. But that would be a waste. We need to work on and improve the Mission statement until we have a Mission that:

1. is understood and enthusiastically supported by the organization

2. specifies company business definition, goals, performance measures, and values

3. provides a guide for the development of unit Missions

4. moves us toward our Company Vision

"Good enough" by these four standards is where we want to start. As time goes by, our performance measures will show us when and if change is needed.

How long should it take to develop a Company Mission? In a large corporation with a number of divisions, groups, subsidiaries—nine months would be a good target for both:

- finding the Mission

- gaining understanding and support.

For mid-size companies, with sales in the tens of millions into the hundreds of millions of dollars, three to six months should do it. In smaller companies, the time needed may be anything from one week to two months.

Mission measures will become the management information system for company operations. Progress on all that matters most will be seen in these measures. Actions will be taken as needed to move results toward the Mission goals and the Company Vision. Changes will be made when and as needed. Vision and mission are continuous, ongoing.

Vision and Mission are not like a planning/budgeting cycle repeated every year. They are forever, as long as they fit the company and the world we work in. They may last five years, fifty years, or ten months. Our measures and our experience will tell us if and when change is needed.

Of the company visions listed earlier, the Lincoln Electric Vision dates from 1906. The Marriott Vision, changing a bit over the years, still retains the spirit of the 1927 original, proclaimed by J. Willard Marriott, Sr., on opening a nine-seat root beer stand in Washington. The word "vision" was not used then. Instead, words like "philosophy" or "purpose." However, the power in the idea of Vision was there, the power that builds business success. Lincoln Electric has been the leader in its industry for almost a century. Marriott is now an $8 billion global lodging and management services company employing over 210,000 associates.

Day-by-day, week-by-week, month-by-month, the Company Mission guides company operations. It's on the table when decisions are made. Mission measures become the control panel for steering the company to its goals. We achieve superior results when we steer by the star that takes us where we want to go. Mission. But the Mission must be right for the company and the times. As described here.

UNIT MISSIONS

The Company Mission is the starting point for creating unit Missions. Each unit needs to know its role in support of the Company Mission and the Company Vision. The Unit Mission can spell this out, including:

- the unit's Vision and business definition

- unit goals

- performance measures

Values need not be restated in Unit Missions. These will be the same as already stated in the Company Mission. Values are company values, that should pervade all company organizations.

Unit Missions can be developed in the same way as the Company Mission. Form a Task Team, and subtask teams if these will be helpful. Use a corporate or outside facilitator if this helps get the task done. Task-team members that worked on the Company Mission will be ideal for Unit Mission task teams. They know and support the Company Mission. They've had experience in finding a Mission. They're familiar with Key Performance Area/Success Factors. They know how Mission measures become a management information system for the unit.

To create the Unit Mission:

1. Use the Company Mission as a guide.

2. Develop a Vision statement for the unit considering the Company Vision and Mission goals and measures. Include in the Vision statement a clear definition of the unit's responsibility—its business definition.

3. Write the Unit Vision at the head of the Unit Mission.

4. Complete the Mission statement by developing:

    - Unit Key Performance Area goals

    - Unit performance measures for each of these goals

5. Organize the Mission measures into the unit's management information system.

6. Involve unit members in creating the Unit Mission and in using the measures.

With these tasks completed, the unit's Mission measures become the control panel for steering the unit to its goals. There will not be many measures (as few as four to six, as many as a dozen). But they will be what matters most in the unit's support of Company Mission, and the achievement of the Company Vision. One example of a Unit Mission is shown in Table 4.

Next-level units can develop their Missions in the same way. Each will start with the Company Mission, and will use also the Mission of the next higher-level unit for a guide. Creating Missions can be continued in this way to the level of work groups and processes. For each, Mission measures become the control panel for steering the group or unit to the achievement of its goals. There will be goals and measures throughout the company, all in support of Company Mission and Company Vision. While many in total, there will be only a few at each decision point—providing the information needed for decision and action at that level.

Throughout the company, measures are used where decisions are made and actions taken. Throughout the company, everyone knows what's important for them. Everyone knows how his or her unit and work group is doing, and is a part of it.

The power of Vision and Mission can be used in company units even if there is no Company Vision and Company Mission for guidance. I have worked with a number of profit-center units and subsidiaries of large corporations to deal with specific problems. Usually, profit problems. In many of these cases there was no guiding Company Vision or Company mission. To find solutions, we first went through the Vision/Mission process described here. We developed:

• Vision and business definition

• Key Performance Area goals

• Measures

Table 4. Unit Mission

Business Definition

The Q Division will operate as a profit-center division of G corporation in the Business Areas of A, B, C, D and New Business Areas to be determined in the future.

The managers of each Business Area will develop and maintain a Mission for their Area, including business definition, goals, and measures, and will develop and implement the strategies and actions needed to achieve the goals. All actions will be consistent with and in support of Division and Corporate Missions.

GOALS	MEASURES
KPA Sales and Market Position	
1) Maintain a leading market position	1) Share of market
KPA Innovation	
2) New product sales more than 20% of sales revenue	2) Percent new product sales, and trend
3) Commercialize a major new Business Area within 3 years	3) Project benchmark reports
KPA Quality and Productivity	
4) Reduce costs of non-quality 10% per year	4) Cost of non-quality
5) Increase Total Factor Productivity 5% per year	5) $\dfrac{VA}{L+K}$
	VA: Value Added
	L: Total people cost
	K: Total capital input costs (depreciation, maintenance, property taxes and insurance, and interest cost of capital)
KPA Profitability	
6) Achieve operating income 22% of sales	6) Operating income $ and % of sales, monthly and trend
KPA Leadership of People	
7) Develop and maintain a participative management style	7a) Annual attitude survey
	7b) Critique in task team reports
8) Provide 40 hours of education and training per employee per year	8) Training provided
KPA Management of Capital Resources	
9) Achieve world class plant operations	9) Benchmarks
KPA Public and Environmental Responsibility	
10) Fully comply with all regulatory requirements	10) Regulatory reporting
11) Always act as a responsible corporate citizen	11a) Employee participation in civic affairs
	11b) Feedback from meetings with press and civic leaders in communities where the company operates

We developed Missions and Measures for one, two, or three levels, depending on the situation. In doing this work, and looking at the recent history shown in the Mission measures, we:

1. identified the real problems

2. found opportunities

3. gained information needed to fix the problems and develop the opportunities

We found solutions to profit problems. Performance improved. Motivation and teamwork ratcheted up to high-achievement levels.

THE SYSTEM OF MISSIONS

Throughout the company there are many Missions:

- a Mission for the total Company

- a Mission for each major unit of the company

- a Mission for each unit in each of these major units

... and so on to the level of processes and work groups. In this way, every person and every work group at all levels in the company will know what matters most:

- for their unit

- for the next higher unit

- and for the total company

And they will have information from the feedback measures from all of these. Everyone involved. Everyone informed. Everyone contributing to making desired results happen.

And everyone is focusing not only on current performance—but also on change. Because the same measures and information flow that tell people about current performance tell them also about any needed change. So, the system of Missions, well constructed and well used, becomes the evergreen method for planning and managing operations:

- building market position

- continuously improving all functions

- innovating the new and better

The system of Missions can be visualized as shown in Figure 4.

Company Vision is the energizing force. Company Mission adds goals, measures, and values. Mission measures become the company-level management information system. Similarly, each unit Mission sets the goals and measures that become the management information system for that unit. Within this pattern, self-control drives performance to desired results everywhere that work is done. Using all the talent and all the energy of all the people can produce spectacular results. All coordinated through the system of Missions.

Throughout the company, there are many goals and many measures. However, for each unit there are few; only what matters most at that level. These Mission measures are not reported upward to the top of the company. Too often, operating data floods corporate headquarters, inviting interventions that are less than helpful. Each level has its own work to do. It's best to leave the information with those best positioned to use it. Self-control at each level reduces waste and maximizes performance.

Mission measures will be shared back and forth between adjoining levels. That's collaboration and mutual support. Beyond that, all that's needed at higher levels is information required for company financial and compliance reporting.

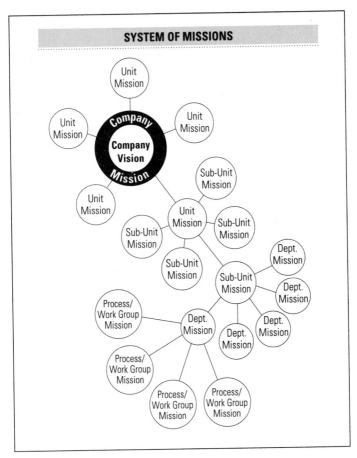

Figure 4.

5

MISSION ECONOMICS

Mission finds opportunity in a changing world. It finds that opportunity in markets, in products and services, in work processes, in technology—wherever the company has or can create competitive advantage. Economics will prove the rightness of Mission, and the reality of competitive advantage. Mission measures in the Key Performance Area of profitability will begin with today's costs, revenues, margins, and profits, and stretch toward tomorrow. At the company level they will show company profitability. At the unit level, they will show contribution to the company's profitability.

The Company mission will include profitability goals and measures for the company. Unit Missions will include goals and measures showing their contribution to the company's profit goals. Then, from the executive office to work processes and work groups, all decision-makers will have the information needed to make their full contribution to company success.

Some examples of company Mission measures for profitability are listed in Table 3. Examples of unit Mission measures for their contribution to profitability include:

- costs and trends, by major cost classifications
- value-added time / total time

- total cost trend / profit center revenue trend

- working capital (controller's department)

- project reports on process improvements:

  ➤ improved output

  ➤ reduced inputs

  ➤ cycle time reduction

- revenues and margins (for sales and marketing units)

- new product revenues and margins (for R&D, and for sales and marketing units)

- prime margin (manufacturing plant)

Mission measures at each company unit empower everyone to take the actions needed to produce targeted financial results. Everyone informed. Everyone participating.

6

WRAP-UP

Nothing is more powerful than an idea whose time has come.

Powerful ideas from the technology of Total Quality:

• Satisfy customer needs and expectations

• Specify and manage processes

• Continuously improve

• Innovate! There's always a better way

• Simplify

• Change

• Shorten cycle time

• Manage by fact

• Feedback

• Predictive control

• Involve and empower

Total Quality offers methods for all of these.

To what end? In our complex world, what is our focus for our particular company; for our unit? Out of all the possible, what is right for us? That guidance can come from

Company Vision

made operational day-by-day, decision-by-decision throughout the enterprise by

A System of Missions

Everyone involved. Everyone informed. Everyone applying the powerful ideas and methods of Total Quality, doing the right things for their units and their companies.

My first job, just after World War II, was in General Electric's Affiliated Companies Department. There, under the guidance of Lem Boulware and Ralph Cordiner, we were inventing what became a new standard method of corporate planning and budgeting. Prior to that landmark work, the traditional budget process was: last year's results plus a little more and better. With the new process invention, we thought ahead five or ten years. We defined our businesses and set long-range goals. We examined the market and market trends. "Market Orientation," we called it at that time. We studied competition and technology. All this wrapped into a Long-Range Plan, usually for the ten-year period ahead. Our annual budget became the first year of the Long-Range Plan, with specific targets for the year. Control reporting measured actual in comparison with budget, with actions taken on negative variances.

We did all this at that time on pads of yellow paper, using electro-mechanical calculators plus a lot of personal interaction. The concept fit the times, and GE decentralized, grew, and prospered. Over the years the company went through several variations on this same theme. The idea spread to other companies, too. Then arose:

1. a profession of corporate planning and

2. computers.

What was simple became complex. What was done by operating people was assumed by professional staff. What was done quickly grew into an annual planning/budgeting cycle that demanded huge amounts of time and effort (and meetings) throughout the year. And as the procedures grew, the results lessened.

Total Quality to the rescue! And much needed. TQM has all the right methods for today. But how to use them? Another great idea, whose time has come:

Vision

made operational by

A System of Missions

Powerful. Talent-using. Simplifying. Needs-satisfying. Timesaving. Motivating. Results-producing. With built-in quick response to problems. And quick adoption of the changes that are right for the enterprise.

RECOMMENDED READING

Bennis, Warren. *On Becoming a Leader*. Reading, Mass: Addison-Wesley, 1989.

Christopher, William F., and Carl G. Thor, eds. *Handbook for Productivity Measurement and Improvement*. Portland, Ore.: Productivity Press, 1993.

Drucker, Peter F. *Managing for the Future: The 1990s and Beyond*. New York: Truman Talley Books/Dutton, 1992.

Drucker, Peter F. *Post-Capitalist Society*. New York: Harper Business/Harper-Collins, 1993.

Gardner, James R., Robert Rachlin, and H.W. Sweeney. *Handbook of Strategic Planning*. New York: Wiley and Sons, 1986.

Nanus, Burt. *Visionary Leadership*. San Francisco: Jossey-Bass, 1992.

ABOUT THE AUTHOR

William F. Christopher is president of The Management Innovations Group, consultants to management. Previously he worked in sales, marketing, R&D, executive, and consulting positions in Hooker Chemical, Occidental Petroleum, and General Electric. He has worked with more than one hundred businesses in seventeen countries in quality and productivity improvement, marketing and sales, new products and new ventures, cost management and profit improvement, planning and budgeting, and information systems and management reporting. He has also served as an advisor to government on trade negotiations.

Christopher is co-author of a technical book on plastics, author of two books on business management, co-editor of *The Service Quality Handbook*, contributing author and co-author of the *Handbook for Productivity Measurement and Improvement,* and author of more than three dozen articles on management subjects. His book, *The Achieving Enterprise*, won the James A. Hamilton Book Award for the best book of the year on business management. He received a B.A. from DePauw University (Phi Beta Kappa), served five years in the U.S. Army Air Force, then earned his M.S. from Columbia University.

The Management Master Series

The *Management Master Series* offers business managers leading-edge information on the best contemporary management practices. Written by highly respected authorities, each short "briefcase book" addresses a specific topic in a concise, to-the-point presentation, using both text and illustrations. These are ideal books for busy managers who want to get the whole message quickly.

Set 1 — Great Management Ideas

1. *Management Alert: Don't Reform—Transform!*
   Michael J. Kami

   Transform your corporation: adapt faster, be more productive, perform better.

2. *Vision, Mission, Total Quality: Leadership Tools for Turbulent Times*
   William F. Christopher
   Build your vision and mission to achieve world class goals.

3. *The Power of Strategic Partnering*
   Eberhard E. Scheuing
   Take advantage of the strengths in your customer-supplier chain.

4. *New Performance Measures*
   Brian H. Maskell
   Measure service, quality, and flexibility with methods that address your customers' needs.

5. *Motivating Superior Performance*
   Saul W. Gellerman
   Use these key factors—nonmonetary as well as monetary—to improve employee performance.

6. *Doing and Rewarding: Inside a High-Performance Organization*
   Carl G. Thor
   Design systems to reward superior performance and encourage productivity.

Set 2 — Total Quality

7. *The 16-Point Strategy for Productivity and Total Quality*
   William F. Christopher and Carl G. Thor

   Essential points you need to know to improve the performance of your organization.

8. *The TQM Paradigm: Key Ideas That Make It Work*
   Derm Barrett

   Get a firm grasp of the world-changing ideas behind the Total Quality movement.

9. *Process Management: A Systems Approach to Total Quality*
   Eugene H. Melan

   Learn how a business process orientation will clarify and streamline your organization's capabilities.

10. *Practical Benchmarking for Mutual Improvement*
    Carl G. Thor

    Discover a down-to-earth approach to benchmarking and building useful partnerships for quality.

11. *Mistake-Proofing: Designing Errors Out*
    Richard B. Chase and Douglas M. Stewart

    Learn how to eliminate errors and defects at the source with inexpensive poka-yoke devices and staff creativity.

12. *Communicating, Training, and Developing for Quality Performance*
    Saul W. Gellerman

    Gain quick expertise in communication and employee development basics.

These books are sold in sets. Each set is $85.00 plus $5.00 shipping and handling. Future sets will cover such topics as Customer Service, Leadership, and Innovation. For complete details, call 800-394-6868 or fax 800-394-6286.

BOOKS FROM PRODUCTIVITY PRESS

Productivity Press provides individuals and companies with materials they need to achieve excellence in quality, productivity and the creative involvement of all employees. Through sets of learning tools and techniques, Productivity supports continuous improvement as a vision, and as a strategy. Many of our leading-edge products are direct source materials translated into English for the first time from industrial leaders around the world. Call toll-free 1-800-394-6868 for our free catalog.

Handbook for Productivity Measurement and Improvement
William F. Christopher and Carl G. Thor, eds.
An unparalleled resource! In over 100 chapters, nearly 80 front-runners in the quality movement reveal the evolving theory and specific practices of world-class organizations. Spanning a wide variety of industries and business sectors, they discuss quality and productivity in manufacturing, service industries, profit centers, administration, nonprofit and government institutions, health care and education. Contributors include Robert C. Camp, Peter F. Drucker, Jay W. Forrester, Joseph M. Juran, Robert S. Kaplan, John W. Kendrick, Yasuhiro Monden, and Lester C. Thurow. Comprehensive in scope and organized for easy reference, this compendium belongs in every company and academic institution concerned with business and industrial viability.
ISBN 1-56327-007-2 / 1344 pages / $90.00 / Order HPM-B234

The Hunters and the Hunted
A Non-Linear Solution for Reengineering the Workplace
James B. Swartz
Because our competitive environment changes so rapidly—weekly, even daily—if you want to survive, you have to stay on top of those changes. Otherwise, you become prey to your competitors. Hunters continuously change and learn; anyone who doesn't becomes the hunted and sooner or later will be devoured. This unusual non-fiction novel provides a veritable crash course in continuous transformation. It offers lessons from real-life companies and introduces many industrial gurus as characters, as well providing a riveting story of two strong people struggling to turn their company around. *The Hunters and the Hunted* doesn't simply tell you how to change; it puts you inside the change process itself.
ISBN 1-56327-043-9 / 582 pages / $45.00 / Order HUNT-B234

A New American TQM
Four Practical Revolutions in Management
Shoji Shiba, Alan Graham, and David Walden
For TQM to succeed in America, you need to create an American-style "learning organization" with the full commitment and understanding of senior managers and executives. Written expressly for this audience, *A New American TQM* offers a comprehensive and detailed explanation of TQM and how to implement it, based on courses taught at MIT's Sloan School of Management and the Center for Quality Management, a consortium of American companies. Full of case studies and amply illustrated, the book examines major quality tools and how they are being used by the most progressive American companies today.
ISBN 1-56327-032-3 / 606 pages / $50.00 / Order NATQM-B234

Fast Focus on TQM
A Concise Guide to Companywide Learning
Derm Barrett
Finally, here's one source for all your TQM questions. Compiled in this concise, easy-to-read handbook are definitions and detailed explanations of over 160 key terms used in TQM. Organized in a simple alphabetical glossary form, the book can be used either as a primer for anyone being introduced to TQM or as a complete reference guide. It helps to align teams, departments, or entire organizations in a common understanding and use of TQM terminology. For anyone entering or currently involved in TQM, this is one resource you must have.
ISBN 1-56327-049-8 / 186 pages / $20.00 / Order FAST-B234

TO ORDER: Write, phone, or fax Productivity Press, Dept. BK, P.O. Box 13390, Portland, OR 97213-0390, phone 1-800-394-6868, fax 1-800-394- 6286. Send check or charge to your credit card (American Express, Visa, MasterCard accepted).

U.S. ORDERS: Add $5 shipping for first book, $2 each additional for UPS surface delivery. Add $5 for each AV program containing 1 or 2 tapes; add $12 for each AV program containing 3 or more tapes. We offer attractive quantity discounts for bulk purchases of individual titles; call for more information.

INTERNATIONAL ORDERS: Write, phone, or fax for quote and indicate shipping method desired. For international callers, telephone number is 503-235-0600 and fax number is 503-235-0909. Prepayment in U.S. dollars must accompany your order (checks must be drawn on U.S. banks). When quote is returned with payment, your order will be shipped promptly by the method requested.

NOTE: Prices are in U.S. dollars and are subject to change without notice.